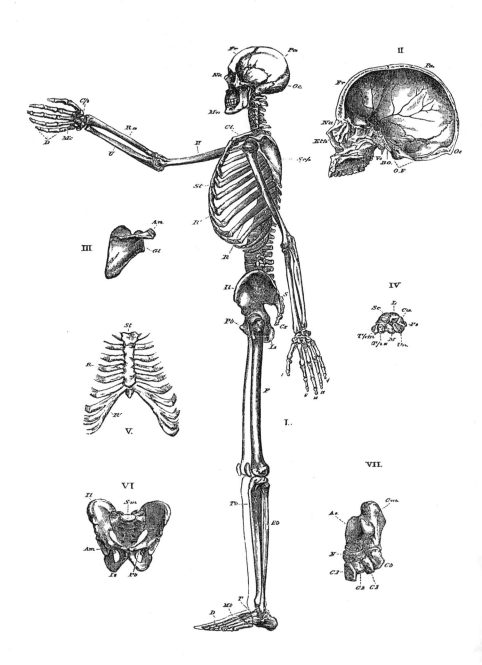

Complete Physical

Shane Neilson

For
Anton —
2013/12/09

of no
use
writes

(stealin
his children
+
the feeling)

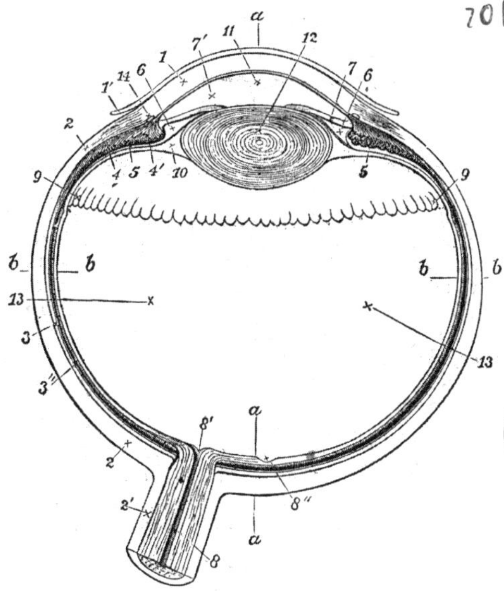

The Porcupine's Quill

Library and Archives Canada Cataloguing in Publication

Neilson, Shane, 1975–
    Complete physical / Shane Neilson.

Poems.
ISBN 978-0-88984-325-7

    I. Title.

PS8577.E33735C65 2010   C811'.6   C2009-906351-4

Published by The Porcupine's Quill, 68 Main Street, PO Box 160,
Erin, Ontario NOB ITO. http://porcupinesquill.ca

Readied for the Press by Wayne Clifford.

Represented in Canada by the Literary Press Group.
Trade orders are available from University of Toronto Press.

We acknowledge the support of the Ontario Arts Council and the
Canada Council for the Arts for our publishing program. The financial
support of the Government of Canada through the Book Publishing
Industry Development Program is also gratefully acknowledged.
Thanks, also, to the Government of Ontario through the Ontario Media
Development Corporation's Ontario Book Initiative.

ONTARIO ARTS COUNCIL
CONSEIL DES ARTS DE L'ONTARIO

Canada Council   Conseil des Arts
for the Arts   du Canada

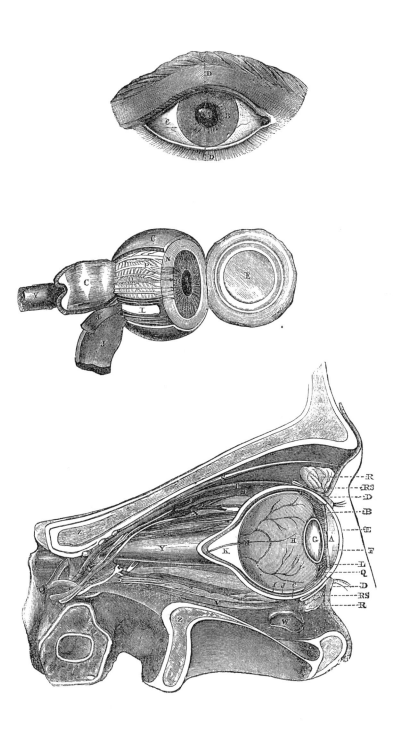

Contents

Part One: White Coat

Part Two: Black Bag

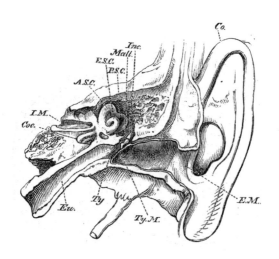

Part One: White Coat

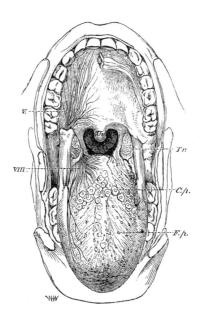

Standard Advice

And there has been love, I have been in love with this,
I have heard secrets never told, and touched when touch
seemed like all there was. I have turned the yawning abyss
into a silk purse, and out of the purse was almost enough.
And to questions I have answers like indemnities, like charms,
like it makes a difference, and I love it when it does, for it can.
My practice amidst the one-horse town and faltering farms,
a usual place where injury blossoms, pain is a boutonnière,
when men know I will ask only if necessary, and women
ask if. And I have loved these loves, I have weighed
them in advice, part salesman, part hangman, the marksman
fooled momentarily. I have no handbook, and my aide
is staying only; if you are sick, I will marshal what I have,
repetitions and one worn stethoscope, love like a stave.

The Doctor Readies the Breathing Tube

Centimetred grace: coiled like a whip,
entering a place where one can sing,
or choke a note. Jiggly jangly, the trip
down the throat a long tunnel, no light

at the end. And if you could sing,
it would be catcalls: hiss, hiss,
and the clunk of machined air hitting
a lung. Whump. O hissy fit,

O life-and-death teeter-totter,
you are messenger only. The message?
Breathe. Hiss. Boo. Spotter
of the poetry of the carina,

weightlifter of air, see-through,
dependent upon hands and necks
and other bridges, you just pass through,
your scratchy sound often capped

by the heavy O of stoma,
I sing of you, I sing of you
loafing in the gurgling drama
of a man about to die.
Will you go in,
inserted like a comma,
like a swan-neck,
will you sneak
up there like a supple snake
in the gargling laryngeal grass,
will you save the wreck
that cannot speak your name,
tongue inverted like a comma
and the relatives asking *Why?*
and you saying *Hiss, hiss.*

The Death of Leo Emberson, November 2006

Leo, at the end it wouldn't have mattered
if they weighed you soaking wet.
Pre-death gaunt, a Tinker-Toy man,
you used a motorscooter, wheeling to
bimonthly transfusions and whirling rounds
of doctors. Lung biopsies, intubations:
you suffered, your hospital chart outweighing.
The doctors kept saying,
longshot, longshot as if they were masters of probability,
dice-throwers on every patient.

But survival was in you. From the wrong end
of Hamilton, you became a Dofasco foreman
and drank until the day you ended up in the ICU.
Delirious and dehydrated, you'd always fight
if there was a fight.

Your wife was asked and asked again
if she wanted heroic measures,
and it must have been strange
for her to hear the word 'hero'
and your name together.
Yes.

It took you cheerful years to die.
You lived to tell me,
between hospitalizations,
that you found life hard, but rewarding.
Your life a matter of application and luck.
Your philosophy homespun and honest;
just like a father's.

Your doctor said, *I've never seen such determination
to live.* And when the end came, you clung,
the monitors beeping, the code team

resuscitating a hero, and your wife,
watching, knew the time had come,
the time when *Yes* is to admit defeat.
She'd seen the readmissions,
heard the team call them, cruelly,
bounce-backs, she knew all the doctors,
and had fortitude to stare them down
and say, *Yes, I want you to save him.*
One muttered, *Full court press,*
disgusted.

But this time, on the adjustable bed,
it seemed like you let go- the tremulous heartline
sloped down, the shocks caused you to jump
lifelessly, the drugs coursed into dead veins,
and the doctors watched the clock and called out time.
It was clear you weren't coming back,
and she let you go, Leo, she let go
and the staff left the room. You died.

At your funeral, I met all the people
you fathered as your wife grimly greeted
well-wishers. Her own full court press:
keep everything together.
Her makeup thick, as it always was;
the pinks and blues a matter of composure.

> There I learned how big a man
> you really were: how that bald head
> and ratty moustache meant a friend,
> was the disguise of a hero, and I felt sorry
> that I doubted your multitudes, and looking at you,
> I knew I needed no more fathers.

The Death of Josie

Pain a concerto in your back pocket,
but you a billy goat gruff, an exterior
designed to break balls. O brassy dame,
Don Rickles in lipstick, wisdom's sore tooth,
wisdom's ass-kicking abuse, you died
and I was not there to hear your crone laughter.

And it would have been sated laughter
that took your lot and pickpocketed
desire. At the end you readied
granted laughter. For no more exterior;
guffaw your perpetual prayer. Forsooth,
solid as a brass bedpost, you were dame

to a pain that spoke from your cigarette throat,
that was cut from your amputated leg,
that suckled on a hag's advice, and for fun
you could laugh patented. And we could hear
inside-out pain, we watched you invert,
the sound that came out a plea.

Hey, they said, *that's just Josie.* My own plea:
that I listened, that I looked down your throat
and saw through the smoke. In verse
I write a phantom appendage for your leg
that you will never hear. I heard you laughed
at last as the paramedics took you, just for fun.

Abscond

You, who talk in terms of electric shocks
that spread from your eyes to pinkie,
you who have a radio for a brain, bad tuner,
you who think in terms of poisons and starve
to stave off the death of Christ,
who you heard an evangelist say was invisible,
but watching like an overeager landlord.

You look at my jacket: if I put it on,
I'll become you; and I tried to get you to expound
on love, I tried to put that straitjacket on you,
I wanted to find out who cared;
But you said that you would die for that sin,
that being alone meant inviting fear to the table
for a last supper, and that you would not eat;
the meal is poisoned.

I thought on love;
on the medicine you would never take;
on shocks that settle in from crossed wires;
on why. And I said, Why not pretend it is the very wafer of Christ:
His body for your body. I was not singing the mass
very well; bad substitute, and you talked instead
of dying every day, of shedding skin like a snake;
your resurrection had nothing of sky,
and you left singing a hymn.

Terminus

How to say to you, *You will die*?
I try not to speak in third person,
mentioning statistics.
I'll look you in the eye.
The word terminal – impersonal –
is forbidden.
I have news, I'll say.
Like an editorialist, I'll preface:
It's not good.
I'll summarize:
All the results are back.
Then, like a reluctant god,
I'll change your life:
You have a disease that kills.
Then, like a chaplain,
I'll pause after my delivery,
and wonder about the real suspense:
How will you die?

Pain

And pain has rocketed in,
glinting vermilion. Try to map it.
It maps you,
an irate tenant,
a mad inhabitant.
It lingers, scenery-chewing,
indigesting, but you are from the old country,
with its flowers and sunshine.

What pain is upset about:
in the hospital, there are flowers,
and mediated light,
and there is no king
who demands *More pain*,
More pain, unless pain himself is a rooming-house king
and his hoary edict voice enacts ache.
But you are just the messenger,
and he might say, yet, *Off with your head.*

Campanology

I've sat, dumbfounded
in my office, as death robs all vocabulary
and grief fills in interstices,
bends consonants and vowels
to its will, and the bereaved
make one long lowing moan.

I've tried to make my own vocabulary,
one with a syntax of comfort,
a grammar of relief,
but all that comes out
is a sound like a tolling bell.

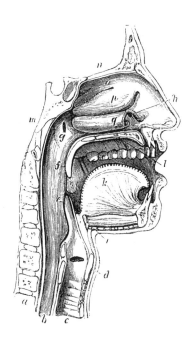

Curing Blindness

I am priestly: leveraging hope and faith and that grand panacea,
love, against death. I take confession and hear about the varieties
of religious experience, which is always love. And I might say:
Always love. But I am a priest in disguise: this ministering
is secretive, and I must say what I can, hoping the soul hears;
and when it does, I tell you verily, that I give thanks and pray.
When I hear of a problem, which is really a distortion,
I might say: *take two of these, two of these,* but it too is distorted:
What I mean is, *you two, you two.* But enough about roles
and conversions in secret; I need to tell you, what I tell you
is like connecting dots: there are points of light,
and if you cannot see them, I will heal your blindness.

Ten Thoughts before the Stroke

Failure.

The sky in ribbons: and you in rearview,

and I have loved in spurts,

the stars have gone,

receding in disarray,

the stove burner on,

you are closer than you appear,

and much is unlatched,

much I cannot let go;

before.

Before (Doctor Monologue)

This matter of what we must deal with.
This dealing with the matter. At hand,
this unconscionable thing, unfortunate,
unfortunate. This long harrumph
before the long news, this ambling
preamble, this circumlocution
like a sated shark lariats carrion,
this preface an approximation
before X marks the spot
and you have a spot on your lung,
a spot on your brain,
dust motes in the air
and you on the chair,
listening.

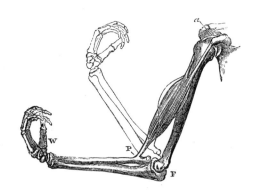

After (Patient Monologue)

This spot. Will it grow to a hole?
Will it spread, a spot-on metastasis,
to embrace a whole body?
And will I die? Is there a chance of that?
Will it hurt, will there be hospitals,
will I have a career of pain,
will the wind-up to what you said
be the last moment I have
spot-free? What will I say to my wife,
my kids? I think I'll just blurt it out:
Honey, a spot, a spot, cry it in the face
of what I might lose. Or I might laugh as I say it,
say the doctor said I have a case of the
Purple Polka Dots. When I know I have
a case of the black holes.

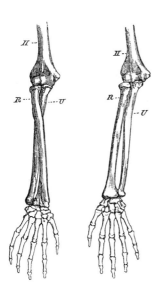

On Diagnosing Alzheimer's Dementia

I'm telling you what you cannot understand.
I wonder if we are lost, or merely waylaid;
where the ultimate question, and your smile
belies years receding into perfection.

I said the diagnosis as if there were sense to be made,
meanwhile there was your husband who said
I'm dying inside. Self-diagnosis makes my job easier.
I look at you, who can still command appearances,
who have not yet receded from the human.

Did you know that, at the end, you may lose your smile?
You will only have a few months to live then,
poets speculate as to why. Doctors sign the death certificate.
When is not up to us, you and me, I'm afraid,
and your husband looks at me with forethought.
You are smiling and social, a perfect acquaintance at a party,
and that there are drugs seems an afterthought. Much is after,
D-day, and the before is taking care of itself in an Elysian field,
or developing in a darkroom, or nowhere.

Do not remember me, or what I say; look at your husband
in the dementia of meaningfully. There are still allotments.
Take heed of what is left, build a life raft for goodbye,
and when we cease to love, there is time to forget.

Old Anatomy Textbooks

Dust-dry, creaky,
I'm smitten by
your nineteenth-century anatomy:
old beaten-down lungs
too long-effaced by bristly
nicotinic cigarettes that rubbed
black spots through the pulp.
Or a cooked liver marinated
in high spirits, or as you say it,
the owner described as *An Over-Imbiber.*
Or the poor man with a dislocated
shoulder: well-muscled, grimacing
as the doctor Cokers the humerus
up and back. Up and back,
up and back; so much of medicine
is up and back,
repositioning,
up and back.

You've been replaced, old diagrams,
by the midnight snowstorm of ultrasounds,
the 3-D colour reconstructions of CT scans,
the preternatural sharpness of MRIs.
But the tale is the same,
the whir and hum of technology
the same as blowing dust off an old anatomy text,
the same homage.

Prescription Pad

5 x 4 rectangle, my name in blocks at the top,
on you I can make wishes come true:
opiates for the world-weary,
antibiotics for the phlegmatic,
caricatures for the vain.

Sometimes I write out fortunes
with a whiff of menace:
Tonight something will happen,
I write, *and never happen again.*

Other times I doodle: patterns of bars
and triangles, scruffy dog faces
and a palimpsest of clouds.

Patients take these strange prescriptions
to the druggist, who always whips up
the same soporific, posting the script
on a wall, where an unfinished collage sits.

I'd prescribe kindness to some,
love to others,
but funny pictures
are all I can muster,
and have fewer side effects.

On Conducting Complete Physicals

If love were a diagnosis,
I would chase it in a field of MRI machines
gone all blinky from delirium,
magnets gone randy.
If the insurance form said, *Check all that apply:*
Love, Lovesickness, Jealousy, Possessiveness,
all of it would be insurable in bouquets and chocolates.

If love were my diagnostic quarry
I'd hunt it like Cupid,
readying my quiver: *Have you ever been in love?*

With a *yes* answer there would be a ritual cigar;
with *no,* a glass of bourbon.

It seems to me a more pertinent question
than the latest burp or cough.
But if there was a diagnosis,
and it was love,
would I order an unlovely blood test
to confirm, would I measure love's telltale bump
with my hands, remarking on colour, border, size,
and consistency?

There would have to be a treatment for love.
What would it be?

Testing 1, 2, 3

A man lay dying,
and no test can say: *this* is wrong.
The man has been siphoned
and sapped
and zapped
and suctioned
and dabbed
and no test can tell,
just babble *Normal*,
and the best doctors in the hospital
repeat the tests,
tests as divining rods.
tests as feelers,
tests as a search party
combing the same bramble patch.
The man cannot refuse,
he's short of breath,
and long ago before the age of test
he ushered in the test
by saying *Do everything.*

A doctor with a coterie
of students approached the strong man
and said,

Let's go back to first principles.
What of the blood cell? It lies awash in brine,
offloading oxygen. The brine carbonifies
with each breath. Little bone matrix,
what's a day in the marrow? And neuron,
how you discharge so magically,
how each elegant firing might be a misfire
(like how did you get here)
and how the tight skin-bag
is such an elegant membrane,
the site of our first resistance.

This doctor prescribed no antibiotic,
no procedure, not even an answer
so much as a song as to what might
go wrong, a documentary on each organ,
and if he could have reached in and righted
the wrong thing he would have,
so attentive was he.

His consult note was written in the chart
in Cyrillic script, *This man has death*
and the doctor might then
have left the hospital for a foxhunt,
or strawberries and cream,
or searched the countryside for good eyeglasses,
and when the man finally died
a message was sent to the doctor at his cottage.

The Test (for Caryl, June 2007)

It's a big one. I heard them say
that it shrinks your head,
glissades like a bubble,
wraps like a bubble,
then bursts your bobblehead.
And that they attach electrodes
to your thumbs and record
every twitch and galvanization.
That they, taking, allow no talking.
That there are needles that break
on your skin, sensate, just to test electrode fidelity.
That the temperature drops,
only to rise like a kiln.
That love and hate and death
are sought, and expressed
in terms of positive or negative.
And for you, only for you:
indeterminate.
Desperate to allay,
to have the good news,
not the bad, friends say
the test takes three days,
and occurs in a basement,
or maybe a forest,
or a helipad,
and that no one smiles,
and they ask if there's any chance of pregnancy,
if you fasted,
if there are any allergies
(the only human allergy: to news.)
They say *Take deep breaths*
until you can't breathe
and then they turn out the lights
and an army of comptrollers
command: *Hold that breath.*

Inside the Examining Room

The examining room door closes.
What's inside: a garrison of troops,
a skating rink, a desert at midnight.
A man could be running recon
on an enemy; a little girl in a pink
skating suit might pirouette at centre ice;
a little desert mouse could be scurrying,
scurrying. In the midst of the martial
bustle, the applause of approving parents,
or the tiny sound of tiny feet, a doctor
might meet a patient.

Recon starts: the transgressions
of the human body against itself.
There will be the story of the little girl
at five years old, how the photographed
happiness has since proved elusive.
The doctor's mind, which is mousy
and makes tiny noises, shines like a lab coat
sun over a shimmering horizon.
It ends with a prescription:
open the door.

Love Squawks through Technology

Dr Gear sits in his home study,
listening to Ella Fitzgerald,
tying flies,
considering cancelling the *New England Journal*.
Occasionally the intercom buzzes:
Mr McGuire has lost a thumb in the thresher,
little Beatrice is inconsolable with a sore ear,
Madame Plante has the gout again.
Dr Gear triages,
judges best how to spend his time:
two aspirin advice,
or *I'll come down and see you.*

The intercom is sublime:
no need to answer the door,
just push a button.
The sound is squawky,
and some patients swear
that Dr Gear told them to *gargle elephants*
or to *juggle toilet bowls*
or, more mysteriously,
to *take the train, take the train.*

Dr Gear heard some strange things too:
that a woman had *catbox on her face*,
that a child was *seething with child*,
that a divorcee with *compression*
needed to *till the field*.
No wonder what he said back
seemed interplanetary-
take the train, take the train.

But one evening a woman buzzed him,
Brrrrringorrahmarahm,
and said how much she *brought her husband,*
how they *sang ditties and splayed,*
how *taking the train had solved*
their conjugal flight risk,
how dinners now are spent at *Erin Village Riviera*
and rooftop shouts are *whoops,*
whoop-de-do's,
and *the taxman cometh*
for joy.

Dr Gear, being an experienced physician,
had no idea who the woman was,
but he knew what to do,
and said *you're welcome,*
keep taking the train.

Christ Child in the Incubator

Immaculate conception a dirty joke
amidst the blood and the bear-down shit.
The doctor says: *Push, push, don't push, push,*
and with the crowning there is no cry,
the neonatal team is standing by
to raise the dead.

Mary wonders:
does the saviour
make no sound?
All this prophecy,
this desert philosophy,
and all I wanted foretold
is a pink boy,
one I could hold.

The cord is cut quickly,
the baby brushed and dabbed
and put on the warmer,
wheeled to neonatal
where god punches his weight.

The team puts in a lifeline,
and another lifeline,
and sucks out some life
and puts in some life.

After stitches Mary is allowed to visit her son.
Listen: preemie baby singing preemie music,
preemie gurgles, preemie sighs.
It's the sound of clinging, of touch-and-go.
Twenty-two weeks,
the cusp of survival,
and the reluctant docs ply him with modern miracles,
shrewd Pharisees with bitty stethoscopes

who wonder: *How much function will this child have,*
will he grow up to love, will he walk,
will he feed himself,
will he be able to learn
and forsake and be forsaken,
will he learn the alphabet
and sing it singsong?

Mary hears them fret about outcomes and chances,
overhears these hallway prophecies.
Her boy, who was born,
too fragile to hold,
too wound in technologies,
too suspended.
Afterbirth stains her gown,
ABCs in her head.
Thwarted, frantic,
she asks to touch him,
this wild woman of red splotches and sweat,
and is told *No, it's too early.*

Her son is blue in the face,
blue in the hands,
blue in the belly,
trying to hold his breath
and machines push back.
His prayer-answering eyes are closed,
and Mary wants to pry them open,
see what is inside,
see if there are answers,
which way this has to go.

The Missed Appointment

Was there a kiss? Did you hit a cat? Did the roads jigsaw,
and you ended back? Did elegy combust, did you take one swig
and decide one more, and now you lie in vertigoed bed
considering stalactites of stucco? Did you get an answer
before I could give one, did you decide that answers are for seekers
and you, one big bawling question mark, could carry the water
one more day? We return to this equation of one,
there being one moon enough to howl, one sun
enough to sacrifice, and one hole in my day sheet
where you would have fit, scrambling, straitjacketed.
What was it? A phone call from an estranged son,
the funeral parlour calling, a door-to-door salesman
came and convinced you to ride away
on his dustbuster of dreams? Or are you on your way,
caught in grief's traffic jam, ready to elbow
(grief has elbows) your way back into the clinic,
with apologies for this and that, and that other thing,
and waylay your grief at my door. I'll try to sell you
on vacuum-sealing what you can't say, and we will
not run away with it, not yet.

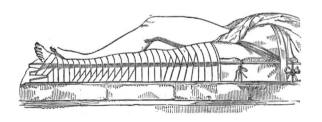

On-Call Song: To My Wife

Three days straight of laying on of hands,
of bleary-eyed testimonials, of being privy
to lies and loves and writing it all down in black pen,
including bowel habit and missed meds,
as if I were the last doctor on earth
and you the last patient.

Three days of not leaving instruments in bodies,
of slam-dunking the pager in the wastebasket,
of sham sanctimony and glam success stories,
What a save, what a save,
the shock-troop surgeons say, of sleepy-slurred interviews
and nonsensical acronyms made of the words Craftmatic
and Posturepedic. It's been three days.
Instead of thinking of you,
I think of how I always wanted this,
but then I think of you.

When it ends, there is no ceremony,
no little skit for me to clean my shoes
of blood, vomit, shit,
and be released. The implacable hospital
thrums, hums with static electricity.

I run out to find it's snowing outside,
or is it rain? The day's half gone
but it's weather, not fecal wafts and fluorescence.
I walk home in snow or rain
and kiss you like a pillow,
kiss you like a duvet,
kiss you like snow or rain
but before we act on on-call absence
I sleep, dreaming of iron men
drowning in Kailua-Kona Bay.

Reading Electrocardiograms

Metaphors are easy. What reading electrocardiograms isn't:
no fingertip sworls, so the police aren't interested;
no long lines or abrupt breaks like palm-reading;
no fuzzy snowstorm screen like a crystal ball;
no crazy QRS dowsing. No one can even tell
that the heart is beating: the lights may be on,
that's all. You need a pulse for that. You need more
than chicken scratch, and what of the exploring heart,
the intrepid muscle with a wandering baseline?

What it is: a detective story.
The private dicks are part of it. There is a gravedigger
shovelling the Q wave's six feet, the long plot of a pause.
It is a history: grizzled, from a Grizzly Adams.
But in the end it is an ocean, an ocean of waveforms,
an ocean that stretches across the basin of a life.
Each feeler P, P of reconnaissance, P of preceding,
leads to the enormous yes of a don't-give-me-a complex,
then the billowing blanket of an ST segment
sloping up or down depending on bed angle.
Bedside, I peer at the tracing

and think lifestyle modification,
lifestyle modification, what every heart needs
is the amplitude of truth. But I'm not looking for truth.
I'm looking for closed-mouth moments and the wave
of goodbye, goodbye, which the police would be interested in,
there is an order to stay within the city,
but it is unenforceable.

Love Poem for the Doctor's Wife

I've held, withheld: what's left in the ragged evening?
Is it love? As a student with a scalpel, I dissected
the squelching old and rubbery young in the lab,
and wondered about what's left over, what was their last year.
The conclusion of my internal organs: it's all pre-mortuary.

I walk through the door smelling of formalin though anatomy
days were long ago, bloodless and like the cartoon skeleton
playing its ribs like a xylophone: jocularly dead. I am led here;
I am led and after I have stood and looked on death
in between middle ears, before the bad news,
awaiting the good, and after the only ministry there is (of flesh),
I have you,

you with a husband the doctor, a wife who has withstood
all this, who has been left countless times, and who holds
this old sawbones at night in the operating room of dreams,
who uses that old wives'-tale salve on my morbid wound,
who is like those beautiful blue tattoos on my corpse's arms:
undying love for Stella, for Gracie, for Saint Joseph of Arimathea.
Or was it Thea? They are all in love, these animated bodies,
and I necromance: I offer all these words to you.

Love Poem for the Doctor's Wife Revisited

Empress of wait, I address you: I do not cherish you less than need.
It is true that in hospital call rooms, I have reached out.
    You were not there.

We both wait, then. I have watched you through the small glass
window
that led though the waiting-room doors, with only a moment;
you sat there like a sacrament. I saw a man clutching his chest,
saw coughing children playing with ancient toys touched
by every possible germ; your hands were folded on your lap,
the ceiling-mounted television did not hold your attention.

I feel like a poor choice at these moments, as a veneer flaw
that leads to interior flaws, I feel as if all of promise
were wagered and leveraged, and before I open the emergency doors,
I think that the doors are meant to protect you, not us,
that out here I am engaged in the losing battle of the body
and that in there you are idealized, perfection: but I grant
myself a moment only and walk through to the basest of predictions,
that you have been waiting, all this time, for me.

The Heart Is Statutory

My statutory heart:
suffused in secret,
kevlared doubt,
has no perspective,
its beat-to-beat response time,
its one ventricle-in-front-of-the other marching orders,
its solemn regurgitance.

A medical school professor said:
everyone is allowed a number of beats,
and no more. But when we die,
we shock it, we drug it,
but the heart is not stunned, it's dead.

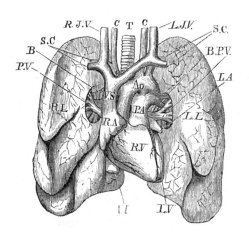

Ode to Stealth

Stethoscope,
you sneak up like a snake,
and overhear doing dirty,
your sinuous S one long tunnel
to a secret. And I eavesdrop,
I see you slither, I listen
to you slide up a shirt
and auscult your garden-variety
divining hiss. A little death
in the summer grass,
the wrong kind of noise.

O divining rod,
O sibilant noose,
grief's earplugs,
love's amplifier,
O silly-sounding S
that's touched a thousand chests,
you've anticipated what I will say,
you are my symbol,
a black scarf,
and I marshal your lanky muscle,
try your bendable will,
but you are not tameable,
you seek what you seek.

Part Two: Black Bag

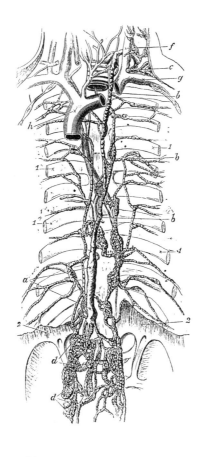

Song of the Most Responsible Physician

At five, I'd play doctor with a toy stethoscope
and only one illness for Mr Bear: *You're sick!*
Now I preside over lives that elope,
over illnesses that hide
until they preside and steal.
They call me a healer.
Actually, I'm an actuary,
an on-call oddsmaker,
the farmer that closes the barn door
after the horse-thief made a home visit.

At twenty-five, degree on my wall,
I looked to yellowed yards of textbooks
for wisdom, and found data only.
There is no preparation: people die,
and I solder silver linings to grief.
At five, my belief: that doctors cure,
that patients live. Now I know the furred truth:
palliation, and survival.

On the job I learned to look the part,
to harken back to five years old:
people want a doctor that listens,
that seems to care, that's sure.
Not a whit in his head,
what they want is faithless understanding
as he massages their fattening chart,
as his ballpoint pen misspells symptoms
and makes a big flatulent blot of diagnosis.

You're sick, I say, albeit in a different way,
and I may care, I may not.
But I laugh at good jokes
and I reach for tissues at teary times
and the word *Expectations*
is cursive on my prescription pad.

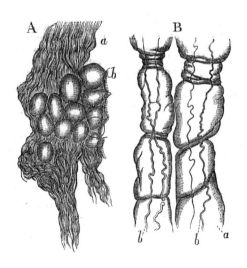

All Pain Can Be Controlled

In the hack-the-limb-off,
pull out the tooth by tying it to a doorjamb,
give the child something to cry about,
cold showers are best, or just ice it, or suck it up, suck all of it up,
punch your dad in the belly as he tightens his muscles,
ten on a scale of one to ten just means a better amount of control,
your lover looking at you and saying, Are you feeling this yet?,
the torturer grinning and saying, Have no fear,
filling the airbag with nails,
stone in the bottom of the shoe for the faithless,
dreams of the euthanasia machine are best interrupted halfway through,
the logical end is death,
kind of way.

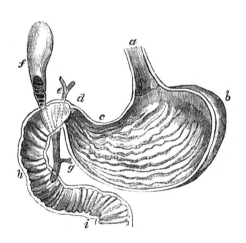

Dr Grinch

I'd like to say that medicine is different at Christmas;
that the people don't get so sick or sad or desperate.
But the god of ailments decided to make things interesting,
that clique of heart failure and emphysema playing patty cake
with my multiple-admits flock. Drinkers drink more,
and when they run out, they shake more.
And the lonely remember more, and the presents
are palliatives, eggnog a chaser. Not to say
that good cheer isn't genuine. But under that veneer
is the fact that compliance strays,
and the dials on pain get turned up.
All the well-wishes and hearty greetings
never decreased the number of meetings
I had with the previously hale, now ill.
I smile and say Merry Christmas to fill
up conversational space, knowing well
that the land of resolutions is just off a spell,
and that's where I let hay grow.
But right now, today,
I hate this season,
with good reason,
as I watch the Grinch
steal health from the little Whos.
Will he give it back?

Fairygodmother, MD

I am a fairygodmother with a licence, I grant wishes
in the form of purgative antibiotics and celebratory sick leaves.
It is better than collecting teeth from pillows,
though I hear children don't malinger or hoard their teeth,
and that their teeth, when ground into paste,
are better than fairy dust for flying,
better than writing a prescription in glitter glue,
better than my best intentions which lately
have caused my wand to fizzle out of fear of hell.

I am aloft on wish power, I am borne on the shoulders
of a sweaty wishing public, and *Wishes are for the wishing,*
I want to tell them, not for the coming true.
But what do I know of miracles?

I know that the best wishes are granted
        by the Grinch of Leave-Me-Alone.
It is my wish to become him, an old trollopy troll
who grants only one wish in his lifetime,
that of a little girl from a Rockwell painting
whose doll was sick and needed a cure for fancy.
The troll, by nature inclined to eat the girl
and use the doll as a toothpick,
for the troll was sick of wishes, and sick of wishing most of all,
decided to spare them both his stomach.
He drew the girl to him, and touched the doll gently,
and said, in falsetto, *I am like a bee, when I grant a wish I must die,*
and the little girl started to cry, her mother was angry,
but it was what everyone wanted: the rag doll was healed.

The Doctor Will See You Now

I parcel out parts of me, fifteen minutes apiece.
I want to ask: were you told you were loved,

are the bills past due and all you can do is fight
with Mike about what was spent on nothing?

Love again. Damn. It's more important than
your sore throat, than your cough. Your wretch

of a day in malady: I rarely fix, at best palliate,
and much of what is left of me is talk.

You are small, tear-stained, and buffeted, with straight black
hair lately going grey. Let's do an advertisement together:

Narrator: *Doctor Neilson holds hands, but not too much.*
And when I cannot fix, a part of me flecks off.

I give the shard to you, so you can rub it at night for answers,
you can suspend them from the ceiling like a chandelier of rubies,

they make great doormats. But they refract no light, will not
warm your pocket, nor are they brilliantly encyclopaedic.

They are finite, and futility chips away at my clinical edifice.
I wish I could join you in the room full of those shards

like sequins, we could make a scarf of not caring,
of intransigence. I could put together a real doctor,

I'll call him Dr Quarter-To, and you will see him
with your beautiful scarf.

Secrets My Stethoscope Told Me

Never take my name in vain.

Never check your list the day before.

Never, never act as if I were the tongue of a clock.

Throw me down at the end of the day and your ears will shatter.

Never fall in love with the sound of breath;
    it masquerades as a wheezing siren.

Never place me against a chest as if laying on hands; I'll talk.

Think of pain, not of flocks.

Ponder the word insufferable.

Dress too well and they will think you're an undertaker.

I hear what the human ear, in its diffident wisdom, cares not to.

Talisman, trinket, tool: I fool everyone as confidant.

You'll go mad if you listen too long.

The Dugouts of Misery

When it is dark, thoughts return to mistakes:
my flight of errors that divebomb all the good
I've done and leave a hole for the funeral home
or the dugouts of misery.

On my business card is a scythe
opening a banana peel,
and my secretary answers the phone with a hollow *Mwahaha,*
When would you like to see the doctor?
There is ice in the parking lot,
but I sprinkle salt on its wounds.

I will think of you at night,
at deepest and darkest,
you are tethered to me by morbidity,
the grand open sleigh
that knows its way.

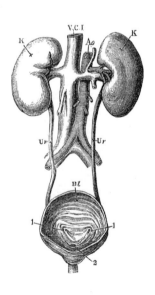

No Ill Effects

I doctor like Charon tends to his staff;
on your eyes the aureus known as tumour.
My heart is a weighscale, gravity the laugh

at death. Drink deep; you will drink. Quaff
like Galen and his sense of humour;
I've doctored like Charon tends to his staff.

Be glad he didn't beat you with it. Be half-
sad; I hear it's a perfect weight of cure.
My heart is a weighscale, gravity the laugh.

My stethoscope opines on your behalf,
says: it's not all that bad. *Stethy, I am sure,* for
I doctor like Charon tends to his staff.

What goes up comes down six feet. Sacrificial calf,
you are in my clinic's sterile abattoir, where
my heart is the weighscale, gravity the laugh.

I'll make the first incision with a gaff
that waits patiently. I bait the lure.
I doctor like Charon tends to his staff;
My heart is a weighscale, gravity the laugh.

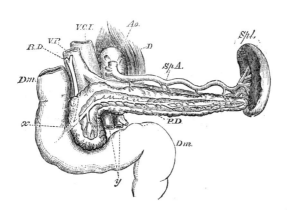

Why We Suffer: A Conversation

How are you, my patients ask,
as if my face were a flag. I say,
You're not paid to hear me complain.
I sit down and listen mostly to noise,
and my flagging attention is like the wind,
disease a windlass.

But who moves the windlass?
Who carries the weight, I ask,
Who is strong enough, I say?
There is more than enough wind
even on a dead-air day, and to complain
is a jest of God, that noisiest of noise.

But perhaps I say too much here, silent.
Perhaps I should just say, *Not at all,*
not at all. And we get up and dance a jig,
I play tuning forks, Rinne and Weber music,
you play drums on your sombre stomach,
the stirrups squeak and the speculum quacks.

Cure? I do not say I quack,
exactly. I pave silence over silence
and stomach as much as I can stomach.
I let you, my windlass, do all
the talking. See me keep time with the music.
Perhaps I am a quacker of men: see my jig.

My Illness

My illness is antarctic, is brittle absolute zero,
is the highness of high places, is a frosted four-leaf clover
wished upon: *is it over, is it over?* Fear, and it is fear,
is left to shiver in the cold: I grow old and awake,
rash, and final. I have crashed and come to ground,
I have outlasted pain to feel, my body hovers
about what's real and flits to what's ahead.
But in this fantastic, this hybrid world
where asterisks attend perception,
when paranoia becomes a kind of love
I frisk with gloves to protect from cold.

Bundle up: up here is a trick of the light,
and I sight what is far, but never near.
Gather hurt like clothes, and grow heady from air;
on a train, it's the landscape that's slow.
I will go, or rather I will flee,
and *you can't catch me*,
I have forsaken care for Hibernia,
the gleaming birds there are few,
just a few crows to curse, a tern or two,
but I see what they see: a man with asthenia,
who steals from himself, whose one cry is elegy.

And it is always about love, warm my porotic bones,
about what is given up against what is given against,
about the poor old soul who leaks out light,
that tattered trick, and my illness is a cold chest of drawers,
my rags inside.

My Illness, Revisited

And it begets cold; I have wished on a frosted four-leaf clover,
Is it over, it is over? Up here in high places, air is thin; I hover
over what is real. There is no pain, because there is no choice;
and what I feel is asterisked, even love, a kind of paranoia
clasped with freezing fingers: too clumsy to be gentle.

I wear five sets of clothes; I talk to cohorts; none of it warms,
fear shivers, and I am not killed, neither stronger.
If alive is bitten, a terminus, a brittle landing,
I'll gather hurt like clothes, and grow heady from air;
it's the landscape that's slow. I see everything down there,
I will go, or rather I will flee, and *you can't catch me,*
I have forsaken care for Hibernia, the gleaming birds are few,
just a few crows to curse, a tern or two, but I see what they see:
a man with asthenia, whose one cry is elegy.

And it is always about that hotstove love:
about what is given up against what is given against,
about the poor old hibernating soul who leaks out heat,
that tattered trick, and my illness is a cold chest of drawers,
rags inside.

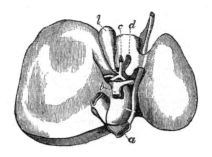

Taking Charts Home after Work

The day-work not done: into a big bag go charts
that are overstuffed with cholesterols and heart tracings
and spiking sugars from too much icing, and hearts
gone balloony. Charts snooze in the bag, kershuffle, and sing
of lives awry in diagnosis, askew in drug, kerplunk in grief.
I take the bag as homework, heavy in hand, and think
the more you love, the more you lose. And loss isn't brief,
I write long notes as life's abbreviations. Kerchink
goes the mechanism of my own care, too brief,
and I wonder what the chief lesson is, and who is chief,
what I can find that is not divine, if there is a link
between that satellite metastasis and that reef
hung like a noose over falling in love, and these charts
are testaments, manifestoes, omnibuses of broken hearts.

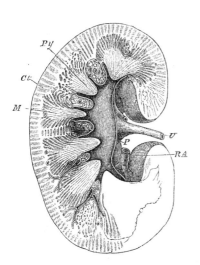

The Law of Gravity

Falling apart, you say? Well. I piece
together your mystery, I find
bad choices, a voided lease
with the words *take care* underlined,

but small print. In my pocket a potion,
behind my back a victual, but answers?
My small print on a prescription:
scribblededibble. It's a kind of cancer,

the cursive path of the dreaded crab,
that snaps and clacks; you will be snipped,
surgeons will give you back to yourself on a slab
where there's a cancer of answers. The crab won't slip,

nor will it blab. And I will leverage
hope and faith and love like a sad acrobat,
like a broker in gravity; but no sage.
Except: all things fall in parts.

Reading H. L. Mencken

Mencken, count the last honest men
as they bear your coffin.
Are you a physician now?

Instead, be my tubercular receptionist.
Bark *No* into the phone
so that the tenderest princess
could feel it seven mattresses hence.

Or, what if you were my patient?
Intellect is not a church.
Too easy to diagnose heart failure
or dementia. You agree,
witheringly.
Put down the phone,
close the Receptionist's Book of Truth,
and disrobe.

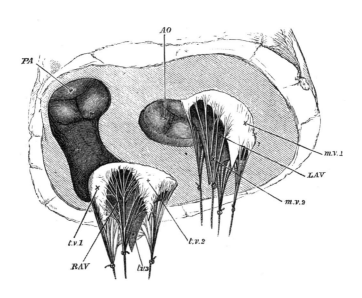

How Doctors Think

A hamster on a wheel.

A needle on the withdraw.

Muzak in the OR.

A surgeon's creased, contemplative smile.

The whisk of automated doors: entry to the hospital.

Washing hands like Lady Macbeth with C. difficile.

Running disease down like a long-grass Sumatran maneater,

and putting the throw rug at the foot of the bed.

Hearing each ward burp out its patients, hiccup them in,
    juggle them throughout the hospital.

With these hands, and these ears, I thee wed.

Take two of faith and call me in the morning.

The statistic of the mind: how much it matters.

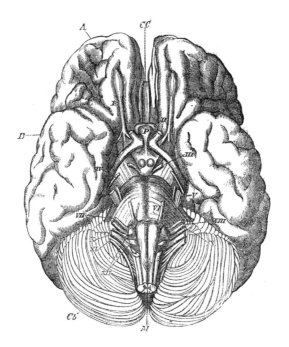

About the Author

Shane Neilson is a family physician who published his first book of poems (*Exterminate My Heart*) with Frog Hollow Press in 2008. *Meniscus* appeared from Biblioasis in 2009, and *Alice and George* is forthcoming with Goose Lane Editions. Neilson also published a memoir about his training as a physician entitled *Call Me Doctor*. All of his writing shows fealty to his origins in rural New Brunswick. He has been anthologized in *The New Canon* (Signature, 2005) and *In Fine Form* (Polestar, 2005.) He edited *Alden Nowlan and Illness*, a book collecting together all of Alden Nowlan's medical poems, and has just finished work on another anthology about what lies behind poetry, *Approaches to Poetry*, which focusses on twenty-seven poets who write about what moves them.

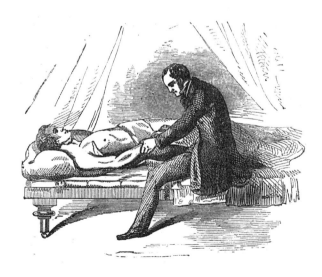

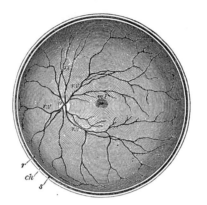